The One Minute Conversion Secret

The Ultimate No B.S Free Strategy That Will Radically Grow Your Business with Zero Advertising Cost!

Nalisha Patel

The One Minute Conversion Secret

Publisher: Janali Publishing |

Copyright © Nalisha Patel 2019

All rights reserved.

ISBN: 978-1-795730-29-7

All rights reserved. No part of this book may be reproduced or transmitted in any form or by any electronic or mechanical means including photocopying or recording, or by any information storage and retrieval system, without permission in writing from the author. The only exception is by a reviewer, who may quote short excerpts in a review.

Please contact www.NalishaPatel.com for permission to translate and distribution agreements.

Printed in the United States of America

To order more copies for you or your team, contact Nalisha Patel – www.NalishaPatel.com

First Printing: March 2019

FREE BONUS TRAINING

First thing first.

As part of this book I have included some additional free bonus training.

I encourage you to go online at http://nalishapatel.com/14sessions and register for this limited time Webinar.

The training will provide additional clarification and extra resources that complement the material in this book.

Please also register your book by emailing info@nalishapatel.com and providing your contact details. One of my team will send you additional resources to complement your learnings on this book.

The 1 Minute
CONVERSION SECRET

Helping Entrepreneurs get their message in front of millions of their ideal audience by leveraging the power of Free Publicity, Media Exposure and also Utilizing Webinars to further profits.

Dedication

To all the entrepreneurs out there that are striving to reach a wider audience to share their unique and valued expertise. Here's to helping you positively impact more people in the world by using the two strategies in this book!

Disclaimer

Earnings and Legal Disclaimers Earnings and income representations made by Nalisha Patel, and www.NalishaPatel.com are aspirational statements only of your earnings potential. The success of any testimonials and other examples used are exceptional results only which are not typical of the average person and are not intended to be and are not a guarantee that you or others will achieve the same results. Individual results will always vary and yours will depend entirely on your individual capacity, work ethic, business skills and experience, level of motivation, diligence in applying The One Minute Conversion Secret Strategies, the economy, the normal and unforeseen risks of doing business, and other factors. Nalisha Patel and www.NalishaPatel.com are not responsible for your actions. You are solely responsible for your own moves and decisions and the evaluation and use of our products and services should be based on your own due diligence. You agree that Nalisha Patel and www.NalishaPatel.com and companies are not liable to you in any way for your results in using our products and services. See our full Terms & Conditions & privacy policy for our disclaimer of liability and other restrictions. Nalisha Patel (and companies) may receive compensation for products and services they recommend to you. Nalisha Patel personally uses a recommended resource unless it states otherwise. If you do not want Nalisha Patel and Companies to be compensated for a recommendation, then we advise that you search online for the item through a non-affiliate link. Do you have questions about this book, Nalisha Patel or www.NalishaPatel.com? Are you wondering if the strategies in this book will work for you? Call at +1 213 984 1012 or email info@nalishapatel.com. We will be happy to discuss your goals and how this book may help you further your business. HealthMastery Ltd / Janali Holdings LLC, PO Box 33105, Takapuna, Auckland, New Zealand

Contents

FREE BONUS TRAINING 3

What is the 1 Minute Conversion Secret? 10

Introduction 13

Two types of Entrepreneurs 28

THE NUMBER #1 Reason People Don't Buy From You 34

Define Your Uniqueness 40

Define What You Want 46

Create A Master List 52

Assess the style for each media outlet 57

Formulate Your Pitch 60

Design your Strategy 62

Creating Profitable webinars 68

Set Your Intention For The Webinar 75

Webinar Content 78

Making Sales Producing Profitable Webinars 87

Introducing the 'PublicityPower and Conversion System' 93

Appendix 97

About the Author 113

What is the 1 Minute Conversion Secret?

The 1 Minute Conversion Secret is the second half of the journey you have already started.

Something in you made you want to be an entrepreneur. You are part of a small percentage of the worldwide population that were willing to take a risk and bet on yourself and your own efforts to carve out a successful living.

Being an entrepreneur can be an exciting journey. But more often than not you are on your own, trying to figure out which parts of the jigsaw puzzles pieces that make up a thriving business go where.

It can be a tiring, stressful and at times challenging journey that radically tests your patience, resilience and faith.

Every day you need to put one foot in front of the other and have a steadfast belief that what you do matters.

You read the books, hire experts to help guide you, study how to market effectively and then experiment time and time again, hoping that your ads or copy or sales campaigns work.

But as most entrepreneurs soon find, no matter how much tweaks and changes you make to better your business, there can come a point where you are just no longer progressing.

In the world of social media and everyone showing their 'highlight reels', many entrepreneurs feel like they are the only ones experiencing challenges.

Let me tell you; this is not the case at all.

Many of us goes through more downs than ups in the world of entrepreneurism.

Your business and message have the ability to solve someone's problem. The impact you can have on someone else's life can be quite profound. It can help people to lose weight, to build a healthier lifestyle, help them to make more income, help them to deal with life challenges and more…

But you can only impact others if you get your message in front of the right people, in the right way, and in a way that speaks directly to them and addresses their specific challenges.

The only way to radically grow your business in this new world of mass social media and online marketing is to get in front of a bulk amount of people.

People want to hear from you, yet they can't find you in the massively saturated marketplace.

How are you going to stand out and be heard?

The 1 Minute Conversion Secret can help you get in front of the right audience and give you a leveraged platform in which to impact thousands of people.

The 1 Minute Conversion Secret will show you how to rapidly gain the trust and massively boost your credibility in the eyes of the right audience.

The 1 Minute Conversion Secret will teach you how to get your ideal audience to happily pay you higher fees for your products and services. You'd literally never have to compete on price ever again or have competitors stealing away your clients based on price cutting.

Everything taught in The 1 Minute Conversion Secret has been tested and proven to work in the real world.

The strategies in this book actually work and actually make income.

In other words; none of this is B.S fluff or filler.

What you do matters, and this book can help you reach more people and positively impact their lives, while financially rewarding your own and help you progress further towards your own success.

Introduction

Why should you read this book and value anything I have to say?

Let me start from the beginning...

It was early 2005 and my husband Janak and I were new to business and also newlyweds.

Literally one month prior to us getting married, Janak had quit his well-paid, safe and secure job to pursue being a small business owner and join me in the world of entrepreneurism.

We had a small amount of savings, big dreams and big ambitions...and basically a dumb yet endearing naïveté about how much money we would make in our first year of being in business.

I was working on building my mobile personal training business where I would go out to women's homes and train them.

Business was excruciatingly slow. I had a drip-feed of clients coming through at the time, barely making much income.

Janak and I were drastically dipping into our savings as we were definitely not pulling in enough money to cover our monthly expenses.

My in-home personal training business was literally one of the first of its kind in New Zealand at the time. Being in a new industry had its challenges.

One of the challenges back then was figuring out how to enter the market and educate people on the benefits of working out at home. I know this sounds weird to say now; but back then it was hard to attract clients and convince them that they could get equal, if not better results working out at home compared to a gym.

I didn't have competition to compete against as such, but I had the obstacle of proving that my business could work and actually deliver results.

Back in 2005/2006 there was obviously no social media and the Internet world wasn't as developed, for lack of better word, as it is now.

I really had to get creative and think how I could stand out and get my business noticed. I needed to make income, fast.

You're probably experiencing the same thing; now it's all about figuring out how to get attention in a world that's saturated with 'me-too' businesses, where you're competing with locals and even others in a whole different country.

As I mentioned, in-home and online personal training at the time were very, very new concepts back in 2005/2006 when I was trying to get some traction in the business.

Around this time, I came across a business coach (Brad Sugars) and his teachings. One of the concepts that stood out to me was the concept of 'leverage.' This was truly a life-changing concept that I want to talk a little more about.

My interpreted definition of the power of leverage in business was about how you can grow your business using specific tools (a leverage point) and implement your business in such a way so you can then rapidly scale up what you're doing.

I also interpreted this as having a leverage point that enabled me to have passive income, where I wasn't trading time for income. This particular topic I will have to save for my next book!

The number one goal in business is to create income that gives you the life you desire. Nothing more, nothing less.

If you're goal is to serve others, you need a good income to support yourself first so you can continue to do your work.

It's easily forgotten that making money is the goal as we get caught up in the day-to-day tasks of running our business, but this is the number one goal to keep in the forefront of your mind.

It's all about making money initially, then about building your business while helping people and giving them the best value through your services.

If you make good money, you can then continue to serve people. If you skip this first step, then your business will not succeed, period.

So back to circa 2005; I wasn't living the life I desired at the time. I was a happy newlywed, but the business was incredibly slow.

Income was completely sporadic as I just didn't know how to market effectively. I was working super early and late evening hours training the small number of clients I had.

I was driving out to their homes in peak hour traffic at both ends of the day, with the rest of my time trying to market and figure out how I could get more clients coming through to create a full schedule of clients.

This leverage concept played on my mind when it came to marketing. I interpreted it as scalability in the business.

Basically 'duplicating yourself' and figuring out how you can get your service and message out to a wider audience. I became quite obsessed with this concept and how it could change my business and life.

I did traditional marketing, including flyer drops, which got me one or two clients at a time.

Obviously, this snail pace of building the business just wasn't going to cut it. Thinking about the concept of leverage, I decided to try something radically different.

I went to my local bookshop and looked through all the Women magazines on the newsstands. I set a goal of being featured in a magazine. I picked out a few magazines I wanted to get featured in so I could get some quality exposure in front of the right people.

So that's what I did.

I went out and I connected with a magazine called NEXT Magazine; a nationwide glossy magazine in New Zealand, which had a readership of around 200-300,000 women at the time.

Long story short; I scored a four-page spread in the magazine. I trained the editor of the magazine over three months and she displayed her before and after pictures, with a detailed account of her experience training with me.

The photos were very powerful in acting as a positive testimonial for my business and along with her glowing review and account of our training together, this feature was a massive hit for both the magazine and me.

Message me on info@nalishapatel.com if you want a PDF copy of this 4-page spread to read and look at. It can jog some ideas for your own business.

The NEXT article that changed the direction of my business and made me more income in three months than I'd made in my whole business life at that point.

The minute the magazine hit the newsstands, my world was turned upside down.

My little fledgling business was literally flooded with new clients overnight. It absolutely blew me away. The magazine came out Sunday night and by Monday morning when I woke up, my email inbox was flooded with requests to join my training program.

Women from all around the country were calling through and emailing. I was very overwhelmed. I had more people signing up for my 12-week program than I could physically service and train.

It was absolute madness...in a good way! I was also on cloud nine and so happy that I had people taking an interest in my business! This experience literally started my love affair with the power of utilizing the media to get a flood of new leads and make amazing money.

This NEXT magazine exploded my little business into the big leagues. I can't even stress this enough. This seemingly small and one-off media feature literally kick-started my business, bringing in so much income that it gave me the opportunity to grow my business further.

I want to stress how absolutely life changing this strategy can. I would love for you to be able to experience something like this for yourself.

In a very short space of time, I went from being self-employed to managing over seven personal trainers to service all the new clients coming in from all over the country, and all from this one media feature.

All in all; I ended up making over $87,000 in around three months, selling 12 week, $1,200 packages to all the clients that came through from this media feature. That's how powerful it was.

I was essentially charging $100 per hour for each training session. I had 1-2 competitors at the time who were running boot camps and doing the odd home training session. They were charging $45-50 / hour. Nobody hesitated or griped about the cost of my services. They signed up, no questions asked.

This NEXT magazine literally forced growth, something that wouldn't have happened without this feature. The beauty of media exposure is that a third person or a third party is doing your selling for you.

The editor of NEXT magazine, who was recognized and respected by the readers, showcased her amazing testimonial and talked up my business on my behalf.

Having a media feature gives you an opportunity to basically brag and showcase your skills. If you did it yourself, you'd appear salesy or as coming across too aggressive. It just doesn't have the same oomph or power if you do your own bragging!

A third-party media outlet or person will basically be your biggest endorser. Let them help you gain credibility and trust.

The NEXT magazine only had about 200,000-300,000 readers, but it was instant exposure to my ideal niche demographic. These were women who could afford an in-home trainer, had the disposable income and fit my ideal age bracket.

It just goes to show that you don't need to be in front of millions of people to have an impact and to make a great income.

After this feature came out and all the hoopla started to die down, I became even more obsessed with the power of leverage. Making that income was mind blowing and altered the way I thought about business.

Having your message broadcast to a mass amount of people at once is the ultimate form of leverage. Media and publicity give you a fast-pass to grow your business. It is so underutilized as there is a perception that only 'other people' or bigger players can be featured in the media.

My aim with this book is to hopefully open your eyes to new possibilities and give you a shortcut by teaching you simple strategies so that you can reach your dreams and succeed faster, showing you that you too can have record growth in your business.

Before, and even after the NEXT feature, I was doing a lot of things that didn't necessarily help my business. I was doing flyer drops, affiliate marketing, cross promotions with other businesses, banner ads, online advertising, word of mouth and referrals.

I've wasted a lot of money in marketing by doing things that didn't bring in a lot of income. Media and gaining exposure are still my #1 way to radically bring in an influx of profits and new leads.

One opportunity leads to another...which leads to another.

Once you've worked with one media outlet, you are viewed as a trustworthy source to other media outlets.

More often than not, any magazine you work with is part of an umbrella of magazines and media. Having one feature will definitely open doors to working with other magazines and news outlets, helping you to continue progressing and growing through mass exposure. If you put yourself out there just once, you can build valuable contacts that can help you further down the line.

Not long after I worked with NEXT magazine, I was featured in another issue of the magazine demonstrating exercises and writing wellness tips. This exposure also led to more free leads coming in.

After that, I was given the huge and amazing opportunity to be featured in the leading weekly magazine, Woman's Day. This exposure was over 6 weeks as I was chosen as the expert wellness advisor on a special Nivea Campaign.

During the very first NEXT media blast, I was a complete newbie and totally naïve on how to maximize the exposure. There're so many things that I wish I had done or done differently, potentially making me another $20,000 or $30,000. I left a lot of money on the table from that feature from not knowing what I do now!

With this Woman's Day magazine opportunity, I had a chance to implement some of the things I had learned from the first big media blast and take advantage of the exposure to make even more income and start training even more women around the country.

From the six weeks of exposure in popular Women's Day magazine, business literally exploded again. I went through another period of chaos and an influx of sales coming through.

At the time, I was trying to move away from just having a mobile personal training business, so I was thinking about how I could sell my online training programs to a lot of the clients that were coming through and whom I couldn't service with a physical trainer.

This Women's Day opportunity really propelled me to create an online program. This was back in 2007 when this concept was completely new and literally was not done by anyone. I had to service women who were coming in from all around the country who wanted my program. Due to a shortage of available in person trainers and the desire to move away from that business model, my online training business was born.

From being featured in NEXT magazine and then Women's Day magazine, I literally changed the trajectory of my business. If I hadn't been featured in these two magazines, I know I would not be having the lifestyle that I do now.

I get to travel and build my online businesses. If I had kept my in-home personal training business model, I wouldn't have the freedom I do today. I would be location bound and liable to a team of trainers.

I can say that having media features literally forced my growth and radical changes that worked out better in the long run.

It's easy for us to sometimes get a little complacent, so having a media feature or having one of these publicity blasts can propel your business and force you to think of things differently and do things you may not have done if you hadn't been featured.

I lay out these examples for you to show just how powerful the media can be in propelling your business. Hopefully from reading thus far you are starting to brainstorm some ideas you can implement in your own business.

Around the time all this was happening, I also became a regular columnist / article writer for several leading magazines, including Her Business, NZ Business, M2 Magazine, and NZ Fitness magazine.

Article writing is more of a long-term game. Leads and results don't necessarily happen fast, but you do get exposure over a long period of time, while gaining massive credibility and connections. This is also something you should consider doing.

Featured as an Expert Advisor for leading Women's magazine, Woman's Day over a 6-week period as part of a Nivea Campaign (see far right, 2nd profile)

So, to recap; the benefits of scoring a media feature / being published:

- Instant credibility booster
- Ability to make a large influx of cash, dependent of type of media exposure
- Ability to bring in a large influx of leads, for free.
- Use of a recognized and respected logo on your marketing materials / website
- Instant authority – in our celebrity obsessed world, any exposure elevates you in the eyes of the viewer/reader

- Drastically cuts your sales cycle down – you can sell immediately to cold leads and take warm leads to piping hot.
- You can charge higher prices than your competitors. I charged $100 per hour for my training sessions back in 2006! Trainers still only charge $60 now, over 12-13 years later. Clients were happy to pay this, based on my showcasing my abilities via the NEXT magazine exposure.
- Immediately annihilate any competition. If you show how you were featured in xyz, the average purchaser is more likely to pick you over the average Joe. Even if 'Joe' is cheaper and has more credentials than you.
- You won't need to compete on price ever again. If you get a few media features under your belt, you can display these in all your marketing materials and a higher percentage of buyers will be attracted to you, regardless of your price.
- Ability to say, 'As featured in….', or 'As seen in….' – ego booster and ability to use on books, articles, website and personal summary blurb to immediately give yourself an edge from others.
- Ability to become a columnist or article writer for leading magazines, newspapers, blogs and websites to pull in more leads and garner expert status.

All this leads to an edge in the marketplace and an ability to differentiate yourself as the #1 choice straight out of the gate.

So, let's not waste any more time. Let's get into the meat of this book! I'm sure you're eager to learn some practical steps for getting featured in the media.

Two types of Entrepreneurs

There are two types of entrepreneurs in this world; Novices are those that set up their website or social media pages, work from a 'set and forget' mindset and basically sit back and wait for customers to find their website / business details.

The other type; Real Entrepreneurs are the ones who work about 10-12 various strategies at any one point in time to get all cylinders firing and to ensure they are reaching out to, having exposure to and dramatically impacting those that are their ideal audience.

Which one are you?

One backslides and wonders why they aren't getting ahead in life. Technically, they shouldn't be called entrepreneurs. They aren't contributing to others as no one knows about them!

The other is thriving, with their business growing more each year and handsomely rewarding them financially.

The goal of any business is to make money. Period.

Excuse me if I sound like I am stating the obvious but seriously how many business owners do you know that are just getting by, constantly working on perfecting their product or service, or even their Instagram feed, but are failing to make any real impact or income?

Basically, the old way of marketing and relying on websites / social media sites are dead. This is one of the biggest shifts that has happened in the entrepreneurial world.

Novices are still focusing on getting up their website or social media pages and making them perfect. They are focusing on that side of marketing and not realizing that they may need a radically different way of getting in customers and standing out in a marketplace that has many options for buyers.

Facebook ads are also getting costlier and harder to get approved. There are a lot of fussy guidelines for Facebook ads and they are getting a lot more demanding and finicky about what is permissible.

Facebook want you to have basic ads. You can't really put in any decent testimonials as you can't promise anything. This all makes for super boring ads that don't gain any traction, eyeballs or bring in any decent leads.

We're expected to produce watered down ads, leaving us wondering why we aren't getting enough click throughs, let alone any sales from our ads.

It's also becoming harder to be seen and to really stand out. Obviously depending on what you sell; your customers can buy from anywhere in the world. Local loyalty is obsolete for so many industries.

And you may already know, you must get a lot more creative if you really want to capture your target audiences' attention….and most importantly, hold it.

With Instagram alone, there's a new expert or major influencer being created every single week and we're competing with these people whether we acknowledge it or not.

The latest 'Bachelor' contestant can easily surpass 500K followers on any Social Media site in a matter of weeks of the show starting, decide to launch the same business as you, and effectively swipe your customers!

We can have the right credentials and have great testimonials, but if we're not marketing in the right way that is appealing to people right now, then we're just not going to get seen.

It's important that we figure out creative ways to really stand out. I teach you two distinct ways in this book to really differentiate yourself from the masses.

Basically, the traditional means of advertising is completely dead. You now need to figure out what you can do to stand out, penetrate your industry, rapidly build credibility and trust in the eyes of your ideal audience, and then showcase how you can help them.

Let the novices wait for people to come to them, find their website, or hope that they eventually turn into paying customers.

You want to be more aggressive about getting in leads, having them check out what you have to offer, have them qualify themselves and then have them eventually buy from you.

Novices also play the numbers game.

Having a whole bunch of Instagram followers or Facebook fans looks great in theory, but I know many people who just aren't monetizing their audience and are struggling to gain real traction in the marketplace.

I'll give you an example; I have a make-up artist friend who posts 3-4 times per day on Instagram, including weekends. She has a following of 98K followers.

She posts pretty make-up pictures, great short videos and tips on all things beauty. She also endorses many make-up and beauty products.

She also gets a lot of free product due to her high follower count. I asked her how much she makes from her Instagram account. She was very honest and said she makes a few hundred dollars per endorsed post every few weeks.

Most companies are happy to ply her with free product, but reluctant to pay actual cash. From her own admission, she said her husband's income really keeps them afloat. Her make up business struggles to gain steady client and her time-consuming efforts to build a high Instagram following doesn't bring in any decent return.

I've talked to several other influencers with varying degrees of follower numbers, and the response is much the same; they get a lot of free products or complimentary services, invited to events etc. but making good money is a lot rarer.

It's like a well-kept secret as so many of us still think we need to strive for a high number of followers to make good money.

I'm not against using Social Media and focusing on building up a following...

But I do believe there is a better way in which to get in front of the right audience and to make actual cash, fast. Still work on all your social media channels, but let it complement higher level strategies that actually make money.

Always ask yourself; how much money are you actually making from what you are currently doing?

This will separate out exactly what is effective and what is just keeping you busy.

The 1 Minute Conversion Secret is all about how to get new clients easily and faster without having to build a massive Instagram or Social Media following, sell over the phone, talk to unqualified people or run costly and ineffective ads.

By the end of this book, I will have shown you two major strategies to quickly establish yourself as an authority, even potentially have celebrity status in your niche if you so desire, so that your ideal audience easily buy from YOU.

Which takes us into the next chapter...

THE NUMBER #1 Reason
People Don't Buy From You

The value of Credibility and Trust in the new online world

Have you heard the phrase, "Putting the cart before the horse?"

In traditional marketing you are basically putting the cart before the horse, where you are trying to sell before you've really proven yourself and what you have to offer.

The number one reason people don't buy from you is that they don't like or trust you.... yet.

Statically there will always be people that will never buy from you, nor like you! It's just a fact. Don't take it personally.

Others may be skeptical that you are the person to help them solve their problem. They are also sizing you up and comparing you to their other options.

You really need an edge in this new world of marketing. You need to immediately convey likeability, trust and credibility in solving their problem, so you appear as the no-brainer choice.

Marketing and sales are all about closing the gap between them not trusting you, to them picking you as the person to help them and actually parting with their cash and buying from you.

That is it. It's simple.

The publicity and media exposure element are about building massive credibility and trust in the eyes of your potential customers. It's about being proactive, demonstrative, and giving potential customers every reason to buy from you. Make yourself the #1 choice.

Which is what business is all about.

You don't want to be busy-busy, investing your time in social media and doing loads of ads; yet not getting the return because there is nothing about what you are doing that conveys trust, credibility or desire.

If you implement what you learn in this book, you'll be doing things a little bit differently from what you currently do, leading to new results.

The strategies I'm going to be talking about are getting free Publicity and Media Exposure, and also using Webinars to complete out your sales funnel.

Do you need the 1-minute conversion system for your business?

You need to ask yourself; are you struggling to set yourself apart from your competitors?

Do you struggle to get in a decent quantity of quality leads that actually buy from you?

It's all well and good getting a lot of people coming to your website, but if they're not converting, then that is just proving that it's not really the best strategy in and of itself.

Do you struggle each month to get leads in the first place?

Are you relying on just a drip feed of buying customers and a drip feed of leads coming in?

Are you feeling overwhelmed and have more tasks to do than there are free hours?

Just like you needed to have a website 10 years ago, you need to be using specific conversion strategies now to really stand out in the very, very saturated marketplace.

There is literally nothing more scalable, powerful or radically more profitable for you, your business and your lifestyle than a well-executed conversion strategy.

Conversion is literally what all this is about, and it really is such an important component of business that a lot of entrepreneurs just don't focus on enough.

So, what makes this different? I'm sure you've read and watched plenty of other books and material about marketing and want to know what makes this publicity and webinar strategy unique.

At this point in my business after 15 years – I started out in 2004— I now travel full-time with my husband, we make multi-six figure incomes from **each** of our various online businesses and this was literally all kickstarted with the one strategy of getting Media Exposure.

Would you like to have this option for yourself?

Would you like to be traveling the world while making a great income? Or would you want to have more consistency and stability in your income, so you don't need to stress so much in your business? Maybe you want the option to make 6-figures early in the year, from one of the strategies, and then ease up on working the rest of the year so you can have more fun and freedom.

After any major media feature, I have women calling in or emailing asking how they can sign up for one of my online programs. How can they get started? What do they need to do?

This is literally their only concern. They are not asking about price, or dilly-dalling on what features and benefits the program has to offer. I convert is less than 1 minute (okay; it could be up to 3 minutes!) as I've **PRESOLD them via my media exposure.**

It's that powerful.

Let me repeat that; I PRESOLD them with the media feature in the major magazine, or the TV Show, or the popular website or news site.

Media and Publicity **PRESELLS** your business to potential clients. This is a major benefit for any business owner.

My programs can literally sell themselves based on this alone.

Anyways, I'm off topic!

Wait, while we are off topic; let me just clarify a point. I recommend you work a multiple of strategies in your business. Media and publicity are the #1 way to radically grow your business in my opinion BUT it's important you still do all the other things that make up business marketing.

Work all your social media accounts, do email marketing, do Facebook Ads, Instagram Ads etc.

Experiment and see if doing Media/Publicity and Webinars works in your business, which I'm sure it will as exposure and getting attention for your business is your #1 job.

Start with this one thing and then bring in the other elements after assessing how it's all working for you.

Ultimately, just try new things!

By utilizing what you learn in this book, you can immediately increase your prices, build instant rapport with potential clients, gain a massive amount of credibility and basically cut your sales cycle in half, actively moving a lead towards becoming a customer.

In the next chapter, we are going to talk about the 6 Steps to gaining Media Attention and Publicity….

Define Your Uniqueness

Let's start with the basics; why should a customer choose you over your competitors?

Grab a notebook and pen or pull up notes on your phone and literally write out what makes you unique in the marketplace.

Too often we get caught up showcasing all the features of our business but fail to show how we are different and better in comparison to other similar businesses a potential customer is researching.

Based on your own buying habits, you know that you also research many options before you buy. You read reviews, you check out their credibility, if they deliver on what they promise and you also look for ways to eliminate a choice.

We all do it; we look for signs of weakness or a flaw so we can click off an option. We want to narrow our list of choices ASAP and figuring out who we don't like is a fast track in doing that.

Study your own buying habits and identify what makes you pull the trigger and make a choice. Think about those elements when marketing your own business

Back to what makes you different; if you can tie your uniqueness to an emotional element that simultaneously addresses a problem, benefits the customer and minimizes their risk in buying from you, all the better.

The infamous Domino's Pizza gets this right, "You get fresh, hot pizza delivered to your door in 30 minutes or less or it's free."

What is the pain point that your ideal customer is experiencing? How can you package this pain point so they can benefit from your business services / product?

I'll give you an example from my own business. I run an online program called the PublicityPower and Conversion System– it helps small businesses learn how to get their own free media exposure, how to write for magazines and also how to implement Webinars to actually bring in profits.

The pain point I am addressing is – the inability to convert.

So many business owners are running Facebook Ads, posting multiple times per day on Instagram and even doing email marketing, but they just aren't converting any of this effort into any decent quantity of sales.

Conversion is an excruciatingly frustrating problem for them.

I package this as – How you can convert in less than 1 minute.

This is what drew you into getting this book, I take it?! I teach you how you can get free publicity for your business to radically boost sales.

So, back to you; what is your major pain point and how can you tell a compelling story around this so that it evokes an emotional reaction in your ideal audience?

I'll give you another example.

Another one of my businesses is selling a weight loss program. I help women who are over the age of 35 lose weight by looking at their whole lifestyle. I address nutrition, exercise, sleep, stress, hormones and the like.

The pain point I address is the challenge of losing weight after the age of 35 years old.

Many Instagram stars are young, and their target audience can vary in age, but my strength is that I am in my thirties and I can actually help them resolve their problem of losing weight at a later point in life. I personally conquered this problem in my own life and have a lot to offer in this space.

What emotions come up when a customer talks about their issue that you are hoping to solve?

Embarrassment – of being overweight, not having accomplished enough compared to friends, physical appearance (hair, skin, teeth etc.)

Feelings of low self-esteem, low self-worth

Fear of losing money or not being a success in business, or running out of time to achieve

Falling behind – need help to be better

Getting older – want to improve in xyz area

Regret – on not grabbing opportunities and want to get focused, need help asap

Sadness – not reaching goal of xyz, wanting to fill a gap

What REAL pain point comes up in your business that you can claim as your own?

How can you shape this pain point into your business's unique benefit?

Once you are clear on this, you can then shape a USP (unique selling proposition) or by-line, if you will, about what your business stands for.

There's no point hitting up journalists and saying you, 'Help people lose weight.'

Boring!

You need to stand out, sizzle with some different aspect that gets journalists a bit excited. You want to make yourself newsworthy, interesting and a cut above your competitors.

In addition to that, you need to think about how you can convey that you are the expert they are seeking.

Credentials, qualifications, past successes; use these things to give yourself a leg up. Media outlets want to work with the best. They never want to get caught out having a source (you) turn out to be noncredible.

Give them every reason to choose YOU.

Just imagine that you and your closest competitor are in a room with 3 journalists.

You need to pitch each journalist on why you are worthy of being featured in/on their publication/website.

Your competitor goes first. What do you imagine they would say about themselves and their business?

You are to go next. What do you need to say about yourself and your business to completely annihilate their business?!

Come up with 3 Distinct and Unique aspects of your business, imaging that you need to share 3 unique aspects of your business with each of the journalists in the imaginary room.

Use this as your starting point. Brainstorm over a week or so. I find that the best ideas come while in the shower or walking on the beach. You'd have your own favorite spots. It pays to have the intention there of wanting help with coming up with your unique edge and then the ideas will start to flow.

Carry a little notebook with you if this helps and start jotting down ideas about what makes you YOU. Why are you and your business awesome?

Let's move on to the next chapter where we will define what you want out of a media feature...

Define What You Want

In this chapter, let's get clear on what it is that you want from your first media feature.

We are all unique in what we desire. Some of us just want the recognition of being featured in a major magazine or on a popular blog or news site.

Others want the leads and the moola.

After 14 years in business; I still personally go for the cash 99% of the time! I have enough credibility behind me now from various features that a media feature in and of itself is just not needed. It's all about the leads for me...which leads to more income.

Brand building and 'awareness' has its place but making money from a feature trumps everything, especially when you are getting started. You obviously will have your own personal goal and desires for being featured.

So, what is it that you want?

Do you want a boost in immediate profits with one off sales?

Do you want an influx of leads?

Do you want the credibility from a one-time media feature?

Do you want to dramatically boost your social media accounts / followings?

Do you want to become a regular article contributor in your favorite magazine for ego reasons and potential leads?

Take some time and determine what it is that you want. Pull out your notebook /notes app and jot down all the things you want.

If you want it all; that's good!

This will give you a base in which to build upon.

Recently I did an article for Entrepreneur magazine. I was featured on their website and was even featured on the home page for a few hours.

I didn't get an influx of leads coming through, at all.

I didn't make any sales per se from the article being out.

I had a few comments on my Instagram from readers who came over to check me out.

This was all completely expected. I knew what I was going to get out of doing the article.

The article took me 5-6 days to write. A good chunk of time! I did the article because I wanted to be able to say I was a writer for Entrepreneur.com.

This gives me a lot of credibility. I get to use their logo on my website and marketing pieces. I gain instant credibility and fast forward my sales process when dealing with small business owners.

So, the rewards were not immediate at all. Sometimes you need to play the long game with some media features, and with others, it's all about the money.

I'll give you another example.

I was releasing a new program called Flat Belly Kitchen last year.

I had had great success with designing a new healthy eating and lifestyle plan that saw me personally lose about 14 kilos in 4 months.

I decided to approach the Daily Mail (UK) with my unique weight loss story, with the aim of attracting a bulk amount of leads.

THE 1 MINUTE CONVERSION SECRET

Daily Mail feature. You can search 'Nalisha Patel' at Dailymail.co.uk to read the full story

This simple Daily Mail feature resulted in over 440 free leads coming in, all high quality as they took the time to seek me out.

I profited over $11,600 in less than 4 weeks of this feature being published.

This is the power of not only getting featured in the Media, but also having a kickass strategy to keep driving sales.

It all starts with knowing what it is that you want.

If you want credibility and logos to build trust, then you will target a specific set of media outlets.

If you want an influx of cash and to gain a flood of quality leads that you can keep marketing to, then this will involve targeting a different type of media outlet.

If you goal is credibility, I encourage you to reach out to your local newspaper and pitch them a story. You might get some new business, but ultimately you be guaranteed an opportunity to say you were featured in 'xx'.

Start with the low hanging fruit as they say. We'll get into more detail on all this in an upcoming chapter.

For now; establish what you want to achieve. Some want credibility only, choosing to only be featured in high quality publications.

Others are not too fussy and want the cashflow straight up.

Better yet; aim to have both!

Just keep in mind that you are always representing yourself and your business.

There could be media outlets out there that are 'trashy' and would quite happily showcase your business and story. It could even bring in profits, fast.

But at what cost?

Align yourself with publications / media outlets that represent you in a good way, reach your ideal audience and are respectable enough that you would proudly share your feature.

Many years ago, I had the opportunity to appear in a men's magazine. They wanted to feature my business and also have me submit health and fitness articles to them on a regular basis. I had to politely decline.

First of all; men were not my target market, so it would have been pointless in the long run in terms of actual profits.

Secondly; I would have felt embarrassed to have their logo on my website or to say I wrote for them.

A media feature or being published for the sake of it is a losing game. Always have a strategy and know why you are doing what you are doing. You probably already have a short list of media websites, magazines and TV Shows that you would love to be featured in and on.

When you get presented with an opportunity or are seeking one out, always ask yourself, 'Is this giving me just credibility, instant profits, or both?' Also ask yourself, 'Does this media outlet align with my values and goals?'

Writing articles, submitting pitches and then actually writing up a story or giving an interview all takes time. Make sure it's worth it!

This leads us into the next chapter, where we will determine who you need to hit up to get published….

Create A Master List

Now the fun starts!

This is your change to decide who you are going to hit up. I always get a rush of adrenalin and a tingly feeling when I submit a pitch!

It's fun and exciting to know that something big could happen as a result of putting yourself out there.

I just innately know when I have a hit pitch on hand and just know, 100% that it is a winner and will get picked up. The Daily Mail article that I talked about in the last chapter was one of those 'hits.

I just knew that the headline, pitch and idea was a winner and would definitely be picked up by the Daily Mail.

I didn't know until later but the article was so popular it got picked up by several other leading websites and media outlets around the world, including NZ Herald in my own home country of New Zealand!

THE 1 MINUTE CONVERSION SECRET

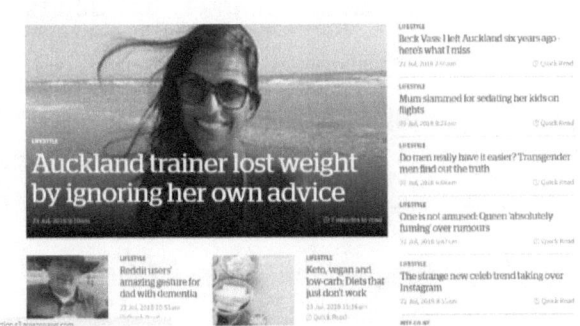

My weight loss story picked up in my home country of New Zealand by NZ Herald after it appears in the Daily Mail (UK)

I had leads coming in from the UK, Ireland, Canada, New Zealand, Australia and even Russia. All from the one media article idea, pitched to just one media outlet. You just never know how one opportunity could open the door to many more.

So, who should you pitch your ideas to?

I recommend you start with some low hanging fruit.

Pull up contact details for your local newspaper, local magazines and pull-outs and any other smaller physical publications that reach a broader market.

List out the editor or customer service contact details — contact number and email addresses.

These 'lower hanging fruit' media outlets will be reaching a broader, undefined market, but don't worry about that for now.

The goal with this is to get some experience with not only contacting various media, but also gaining experience with being featured and having a few runs under your belt.

I'm mixing my analogies here, aren't I?!

Anyway, back to a tree analogy; start with lower hanging fruit and then you can move your way up, ensuring you have the experience to maximize the exposure.

If I had known what I know now about having a media blast, I would have made at least double what I did with the NEXT magazine blast. I just had no clue as to what I was doing.

So, I recommend you start small and broad, not worrying too much about financial rewards, and just use it for the experience.

After you have compiled this list, move up the 'tree' and start thinking about which mid-level 'fruit' you need to target. For now, you are just gathering information.

After this, move up to a higher level 'fruit'; I'm talking, Entpreneur.com, Yahoo, your country's biggest News site, major nationwide /international magazines like Women's Health, Success magazines – you get the idea. Tailor this to suit your niche and ideal market.

Now the fun part; I want you to go to your local bookstore or library and look at the range of magazines. Buy or borrow the magazines that appeal to your target audience.

So, what do your ideal audience read?

If you are in the health and wellness industry, you would buy Women's Health, Shape, Prevention and smaller weekly women's magazines like Woman's Day, Us magazine, That's Life etc. and even smaller magazines that serve specific niches, like Body and Soul Magazine, Vegan magazines and the like.

Then move online and list out the equivalent low, mid and higher hanging fruit of websites, blogs, magazines and news sites you desire to contact.

Gather key contact details and be prepared to jump on the phone to call them.

Utilizing Instagram and Twitter

In addition to your physical and online media outlet hunting, I recommend you cross reference the names / writers that you gather and hunt them down on Instagram and Twitter.

Oftentimes reporters and journalists write on their twitter or Instagram feeds that they need xyz (i.e. possibly you) for a story they are working on.

Friend them / follow them and then start building a relationship with them.

Direct message them or comment on their posts. You can either wait for them to need someone like you for a story, or you can be a bit more aggressive and hit 'em up first and pitch them your idea. We'll talk Pitches soon in an upcoming chapter.

Your call! You decide how aggressive you want to be and if it's appropriate. I've hit up a couple of journalists / writers with ideas through Instagram and heard crickets.

I have had small success with one story where a writer wrote on Twitter that she needed to interview a Digital Nomad. Fitted me perfectly so I immediately wrote to her and she quoted me on a blog.

No matter what; test the temperature. You don't want to come across me-me-me or too pushy. Play the long game and avoid burning any bridges. The publishing world is surprisingly quite small, especially if you focus on one country.

This leads us directly into the next chapter where will talk style of media.

Let's move on.

Assess the style
for each media outlet

Okay, so you have two options when dealing with the meal; you can either pitch a media outlet articles you want to contribute, or you can pitch a one-off media piece / blast.

In this book, I am focusing more on one-off media pitches.

You need to study the media outlet in question for ideas on how they write or showcase their material.

For example; several years ago, I pitched an idea to offer a fitness package to a fitness magazine here in NZ that was very popular at the time.

It would be a one-off package promotion. I assessed the style of the magazine and determined what their readers would be interested in with Fitness Package and made sure it contained things that they would find beneficial.

As I was running an in-home personal training business at the time, the readers of Fitness Life magazine were my ideal target audience.

I tailored (i.e. made up and then designed) a package to appeal to this readership.

My offer of a Fitness Package was very appealing to the editor of the magazine, so I ended up with a one-page advertisement of it, plus a cover blurb featuring the package and my business name.

As you can see in the below image; they had a billboard done up and my fitness package was the main superstar!

Exciting right?

Now; if I had approached the magazine and had offered them a business coaching package to help any of their readers in business, I doubt the offer would have been accepted.

I'm sure they had business people as their readers, and even if my offer was high value; it just didn't fit in this instance.

Fitness Life Magazine ran my fitness package as their main headliner

Common sense, but easily overlooked. As I said; assess each and every one of the media outlets you plan to pitch to and pitch accordingly.

I've mentioned the Daily Mail article earlier in this book.

The topic/pitch was, '**As a Personal Trainer, I gained 30lbs from Traveling the World and Had to Do the Opposite of Everything I Taught my Clients to Finally Lose 28lbs in 16 weeks!**'

This appealed to the style of writing on Daily Mail. It wouldn't appeal to Women's Health or Prevention Magazine, for example. With experience you'll easily determine how best to craft a pitch for each media outlet.

Ultimately just know that you need to do your homework. Spend the time on the front end working on several pitch ideas and then craft them to each media outlet, one by one.

This brings us to the next chapter where we will talk more about Pitches.

Formulate Your Pitch

By now you should have a shortlist of media outlets, on and offline, that appeal to you and that reach your ideal audience.

So now it's time to get your message out to journalists or writers. So how do you craft your message?

The biggest thing to keep in mind is that these journalists/writers/editors really couldn't care less about your business…BUT they really only care about presenting you to their readers/viewers so that these people can benefit.

In other words; cut out any me-me-me style of pitch of requests and focus on what you can offer their readers/viewers.

That is what it is all about.

You probably notice this yourself; you could be reading a blog or an article on a site and it is too 'I' or 'Me' orientated. With these types of articles, you probably click off pretty fast.

We are all scrolling, surfing and skimming to get to the bits on how we personally can benefit. We don't have time to waste!

So, journalists /writers /editors are looking for what can benefit their readers /viewers.

Give this to them. Make their lives easier.

When formulating your pitch, focus on these:

What is my unique point of difference (see chapter 1) – how can I convey how I am different from others in my niche?

Why am I newsworthy to this particular media outlet?

What benefit am I offering their readers / viewers?

How can I convey that I am the expert they are seeking?

What images, resources, links etc. can I provide to strengthen my pitch?

Ultimately show how you are of benefit to the media outlets' readers/viewers. If you did just this, then you will have success.

Design your Strategy

By now you should have a list of media outlets you want to target and the type of pitches you will send out.

Before you pull the trigger and start hitting up various media outlets, I suggest you get a strategy together.

Know what your moves are to help you stay focused and on point.

Start with lower level media outlets and work your way up, to get some rungs on the ladder before working your way up to outlets with a higher reader or viewership.

This will give you the opportunity to experience what it's like to have media coverage and to assess which parts of your sales strategy you need to tweak to ensure maximum results.

Be relentless. Often, a media outlet will respond to you when the timing is better for them. You can either keep pitching a variation on your story to them or following up on the original pitch.

If all goes well, chaos will ensue!

You might never be prepared for your first media blast. I definitely wasn't, and even now, all these years later, I still find that it can get pretty crazy.

Be prepared to get inundated with several new leads. Depending on the publication and the type of media exposure, you could literally be run off your feet.

Are you and your business prepared for many calls, emails and actual sign ups/purchases? Can you handle the increased work load?

What measures do you have in place to ensure your website, landing pages and resources are all up to date and capable of handling a possible influx of new clients / buyers?

If you're new to getting publicity for your business, you might be surprised at just how many new inquiries and leads will come through from one just feature.

Be prepared for immediate sales, along with a lot of inquiries. Be prepared to handle extra customer service, fulfilling sales and knowing how to capitalize on the feature.

You sometimes only get one shot to maximize your media feature / publicity exposure so prepare as best you can.

The NEXT article was like lightning in a bottle; the experience has never been repeated. So many factors came into play to make that feature a massive financial and business success.

As I mentioned; my business was one of the first of its kind back then when the article came out. It was novel and different and so demonstrative in showing the benefits of working out at home.

The editor did an amazing job of showcasing my expertise and her ultimate results. All these factors meshed together to produce one of, if not, my most successful media campaign.

I hope you are getting excited at what possibilities and opportunities lie ahead for you and your business if you work a Media Strategy into your business. It really is exciting!

If you are interested in having me walk you through how to go about getting a media feature for your business, let me just tell you briefly about my online course, 'PublicityPower and Conversion System' -

I will personally walk you through the techniques and strategies you'll learn on the online program, even giving you a head-start with my best contacts in the media and publishing industry. This is invaluable!

It's a very detailed program on each part of getting media, what to do before, after and during your media feature to maximize sales.

I'll also walk you through how to become an article writer or columnist for a leading publication / magazine.

I stand by the fact that everything I teach is real world and proven techniques that have actually brought in results.

See the Appendix for all the various media blasts and exposure I've had over the years and you'll see some examples on some of the media outlets I can help you get into yourself.

None of this is Theory! All strategies have been PROVEN to actually work in the real world.

Let's move on to the next chapter where I talk to you about creating Profitable Webinars to complement and enhance your sales funnel.

PART TWO – BONUS

Creating
Profitable webinars

The reason I have included Webinars as a bonus conversion tool in this book is that they really can be powerful in converting cool or warmish clients to converted clients when added to your sales funnel.

I think of Webinars as a 24/7 'salesman', which can successfully do your selling for you. You can set them up, so they run while you are out, on holiday, sleeping etc. Done right they can be very powerful.

Using webinars also helps set you apart from the mass market. So many entrepreneurs know they should be doing webinars in their business, but not many actually do them! Or I should say; not many do them successfully, which leads them to abandoning them.

Webinars are perceived as taking a lot of time to set up. And yes, they can be time consuming if you don't have a blueprint to follow or have never done them before.

But if you just pull the trigger and learn how to set just one up; you will be able to churn webinars out regularly.

Webinars also beautifully complement any media features you may be featured in and these two strategies can work together and move you closer to phenomenal success in your business, while impacting your bottom line.

I know you've probably heard that said before, but I guarantee that if you employ just one of these strategies, you'll see a massive difference in your business.

The first strategy as I've talked about is how to easily convert clients or get customers without ever having to literally pick up the phone, talk to potential buyers, pay for advertising or even compete with others in your saturated marketplace ever again.

Gaining the right kind of publicity for your business can be that powerful.

I have replicated this strategy many times over in my own business using various media features. See the Appendix at the end of this book for various media features and how it impacted the business. It should jog some ideas that you can use yourself in your own business.

In this chapter we'll be talking about using Webinars to bring in cold leads, and to also rapidly convert warm leads.

I will address some key elements that can help get you thinking about their value and how you too could add them to your own sales funnel if you so desire.

Let me give you a real-world example of how I've used webinars;

For my Daily Mail feature, which was then picked up by the NZ Herald, I literally didn't talk to one purchaser on the phone or in person.

My aim with the Daily Mail feature was to make a massive amount of sales in a short period of time for my new health and weight loss program.

I was selling a base level $247-297 online weight loss program, and a higher-level coaching one for $997.

I had about 442 leads come through from the feature. Not one purchaser that came through from the Daily Mail (and NZ Herald) needed to talk on the phone, nor did they question the price or 'have to think about it.'

I sold my base level program to approximately 40 people, and only had 2-3 people ask some basic questions about health and fitness to assess how they would progress on the program if they were to buy it.

The 3 people that paid $997 were COLD Leads. I had never communicated with them before. They were not on my database, nor social media and they had never heard of me prior to the Daily Mail (and NZ Herald) article coming out.

This is how powerful getting into the media can be! That one story conveyed everything; my credibility, my story, what solution I could offer them, all packaged up and aligned with something they already consumed and trusted (Daily Mail and NZ Herald).

As you will learn when you start getting your own media and publicity features; you will gain instant credibility and instant trust, which leads to faster sales and profits.

I hope this excites you and has you imagining the possibilities for yourself and your business if you were to implement what you have learnt so far, so you can get your own publicity features to radically grow your own business.

It can be really exciting!

As I mentioned previously, I had over 440 high quality leads come in within 4-5 days of the feature coming out. The bulk of the sales were made within 2-3 days of the media feature being published, BUT there were a few sales made over the course of 3-4 weeks.

In other words, a percentage of the people that did end up buying didn't buy straight away.

What was my secret weapon in converting this percentage of people?

WEBINARS (in this case, two webinars).

I qualified the leads that came through and introduced them to my webinar – '7 Myths of losing weight' and 'How Sleep impacts your weight loss progress'.

I should have known better from past experience, but I didn't expect such a big response from the Daily Mail feature. It exceeded my expectations.

I had to literally design, create and set up these webinars **within days** of the Daily Mail article coming out!

Since I had done webinars before, I had already devised a rapid system / template for churning out high converting webinars, fast, making sure to touch on persuasive elements to convert a lot higher.

The webinars I ran weren't even live. I recorded them a few days after the feature came out. I wanted a way to market to the leads that explained a little more about how I could help them.

The webinars are both now evergreen and play when it suits the registered users and their ideal time zone.

The beauty of creating webinars are that you can re-use them again and again and again...for infinity. My #1 tip; in business always look for leverage points to save you time, whilst bringing in profits.

If you're thinking about going global or even having an online business, then using webinars is one strategy you absolutely need to convince or attract clients to buy from you. Your webinar will do the talking for you.

There are several things that make Webinars so powerful:

People sign up for them knowing that they need to spend time viewing them – i.e. they are committing to listening to you for 20-30 minutes. minimum. You have their attention for a chunk of time.

Cold or Warm leads get to listen to your voice, hear your personality, possibly see you, your mannerisms and get a feel as to whether they even like you.

Webinars allow you the time to educate and then actually sell. You get to take your time and walk through your product/service; something email, quick videos on social media or pictures on Instagram or Facebook just can't convey.

You get to sell! There is an expectation there from registrants. They are ready and primed to listen to you and know they will get sold to.

Well most people do; you get the odd weird email from 'offended' viewers who are shocked that you are selling them something at the end of the webinar.

Ridiculous! Remember; you are a business. Your #1 job is to sell your quality service or product. Nothing more, nothing less.

If you don't make money, you'll be useless. Your business will fail, and you won't be helping anyone. I can't tell you how many entrepreneurs I talk to that are afraid to ask for the sale or are too shy to sell.

If anyone has a problem with you selling them something; tell them take their business elsewhere. Trust me; you don't want these types of people as customers. They will make your life hell. Been there, done that. Absolutely not worth your time. You don't want these peoples' money.

Ok, rant over!

Back to Webinars. You get to run Webinar-only specials – these time limited specials really get the fire under truly interested parties' butts so that they buy on the spot.

In your webinar you get to showcase yourself, your voice, images you want to share, even videos, and if done live, you get to do a live Q & A.

Webinars are super powerful when done right and are another link in your sales funnel.

Let's dive into some details….

Set Your Intention For The Webinar

Should you even run webinars in the first place? If you have value to offer and can deliver it in an interesting and fresh way, then you should absolutely be adding webinars to your marketing tool box.

Just as you did with your Media Pitches, you need to decide first what is it that you want from your webinars.

Do you want to push people who are already on your database further down your sales process, with the aim of selling them via the webinar?

Are you marketing your webinar to cold leads; for example, pushing your webinar through Facebook ads to bring in new leads and not necessarily selling them anything?

Depending on which option you choose (you may alternate between both); you will need to tailor your webinar to suit.

Basically, if you are setting up a webinar to viewers who already know you, you can skip the 'getting to know you' part and focus on one key topic.

For cold leads; i.e. viewers who have literally never heard of you before but took interest in your topic, you need to lay out from the get-go why they should listen to you.

This is where any media features or publicity you have will give you a leg up. Cold leads will stick around if they perceive you as an expert, or even as a cool person who's piqued their interest.

Name drop that you were featured in xyz, and the reason and you will capture their attention, especially if it relates to the solution they are seeking.

Highlight this from the very, very start. From your own webinar viewing habits, you will know that you are more likely to click off the webinar if the host doesn't convey any sense of expertise. We may also click off if we don't like their face, voice, attitude...there are many reasons! Some are out of our control, but some factors we can boost.

We are all short on time and fussy with what we spend our precious time on. So, why should someone listen to YOU?

Spell this out from the very start and covey a lot of benefit to the viewer. So many amateur webinar hosts harp on about themselves and tell super boring stories. They are probably stumped as to why their webinars aren't making any sales.

THE 1 MINUTE CONVERSION SECRET

Focus on the viewer as your set your webinar intention AND design it based on this.

Why should they spend their time listening to YOU?

Webinar Content

As discussed in the previous step; always focus on the viewer.

Why should they listen to you and why is the topic of interest to them?

Ask yourself; who is my target audience? Get crystal clear on this so you can deliver a specific solution to a specific audience.

Is your ideal webinar viewer a new audience member or a current one based from your database?

What will the webinar topic be that you know your database /ideal audience are struggling with?

Webinar Topic

Decide on three different and specific topics that address a problem your database / potential audience are struggling with, and that you can provide a solution for. It's always good to have several winning topics on hand.

Remembered at each step as you design the webinar to ask yourself; how can I keep adding value to my listeners and what is in it for them?

Once you decide on three different and specific topics, narrow it down even more for each idea and focus on ONE key element to address.

For example; you could have a topic of, "How to gain free leads for your business."

You would then narrow this down to, "How to gain free leads using just LinkedIn."

Or a webinar I could run would be, "How to gain 1000 free leads using free media exposure for your business."

When you are designing your first webinar, simplicity is key. If you have too many focuses, you'll more likely get overwhelmed and get turned off producing webinars.

Make your first webinar really basic, on the short side, and loaded with lots of value. You can always add more for later editions, but your first one should be done fast and easily.

As you run more webinars, you'll be able to refine your topic based on what attendees ask, which topics garner the most registrations and also what your database requests.

Style of webinar

There are various types of webinar styles to choose from; Q & A, power-point only, video with screenshare and sharing the webinar with others (interview style, panelists) to name a few.

Also, you need to choose between doing them live, recorded (then run continuously) or a mix of both over time.

I suggest for your very first webinar to do a Power Point webinar and to pre-record it. You can show your face at the start if you desire, and then basically have webinar attendees watch and listen to your power point presentation with you talking along to the points on the slides.

This is fast, basic and the power point slides will help you narrate your key points.

This is personally my favorite style. I prefer recorded over live, unless there is a specific reason I need to go live. My very first webinar was live and done when we lived in Los Angeles for three months in an Airbnb. I had a handful of people on it, one of which was my Dad! I was super nervous, and the internet kept cutting out.

It was awful, long and winded, virtually pointless as I saw attendees drop off (including my Dad!) not too long into it and was nerve-wracking.

I usually do a webinar once live and then use that as an evergreen recording. It saves me a ton of time, and still produces sales. I'm sure I would make more if I did them live, especially with a live Q & A at the end, but for now this style suits me and my goals.

Video is also great, as is Q &A and interviewing a guest.

You too will find that your preference will switch and change over time. You just need to try them.

Start and then experiment

As mentioned above, pick one style, learn the ins and outs of doing webinars and then you can experiment and see which style of webinar works for you. You'll only get better with practice and the deliberate tweaking of factors to see what works for you and your business.

I recommend that your first webinar be pre-recorded. This way you just get comfortable talking for so long. I remember shooting my first recorded webinar and I was so nervous! I nearly lost my voice as I wasn't used to talking for so long. Also just knowing that people were eventually going to listen to the webinar made me self-conscious. A live webinar is a whole other level of nerves. Start small and work your up!

For one of my first webinars, I ran a Facebook ad and only 7 people tuned in to watch!

I had zero sales from this webinar, but it was a great learning experience. I was proud of myself for getting a webinar up and giving it a go, but obviously very disappointed that I had zero sales. My expectations were just too high and unrealistic for my initial webinars.

I kept experimenting and I ran several webinars back to back just to measure different things. On the sixth webinar I experimented with, I had refined it all a bit more and I had around 40 people tune in to watch the Webinar.

I ended up with one sale. I was selling a $497 program, so for running this webinar it wasn't a bad return. This type of return is obviously not the best thing for building a business in the long run though!

For my 10th webinar, I really kind of mastered the art of persuasion and I utilized my media features to showcase not only why my online training programs were awesome, but also my credibility and how I could actually help them.

With this particular webinar I had around 65-70 people tuning in and I ended up with 7 sales, profiting $6,979. This was from a 45 minutes webinar. Once you get better at doing webinars, you really can get to the nuts and bolts of it and start selling a lot faster and easily by having a really streamlined webinar process.

A lot of people are throwing webinars out there; some convert and some don't. There is obviously a right and wrong way to run webinars. Have you ever watched a webinar, invested time in it and then at the end thought, 'What in the world did I get from that?'

The key with a successful webinar is to convey to the viewer why YOU are the person to buy from, while also highlighting, talking about and ultimately showing how you are the solution to their problem.

That is your #1 job. People fail with webinars because they haven't touched on all these points.

With Media Exposure, you are essentially sealing the deal. People want to work with and get helped by someone who is trustworthy and can prove that they are capable of doing the job.

Get media exposure, rack up the credibility and then run webinars that allow you the time to convey all this and to show off, brag and highlight how you are an expert and the one to choose. The beauty of webinars is that you can use them to warm up cold leads and keep plugging them in your sales funnel to eventually convert more and more people down the line.

Let me give you another example;

My most successful webinar to date was a $21,600 one, marketed to my existing database.

These were people that had been on my list for a while, had opened a few emails here and there. They may have bought one of my books, done one of my other programs, or done a consulting call with me.

Running webinars to your own database, assuming they are warm leads, is one of the fastest ways to boost your business.

This $21,000 webinar was a big deal and literally opened my mind up to the power of webinars added to a sales funnel.

To celebrate this big win, Janak and I flew to the Rhodes Island in Greece (we were already in Turkey) and had an awesome time snorkeling and eating in one of our most favorite countries in the world. It was a nice reward after many flops!

I've since used webinars to rapidly convert new and existing leads into more profits. You can have various webinars highlighting different things that you sell so you can sell to existing clients, or you can sell to brand new leads as well.

One of the most important things that I recommend you do with webinars is to set them up, so they run automatically and perpetually (evergreen), so you're constantly generating cash from the work that you've done, and nothing goes to waste.

This is the epitome of leverage. Let people in different time zones 'attend' when it suits them. Throw in some live webinars every so often, and you'll eventually be building a strong sales funnel.

Full disclosure; as mentioned when you purchased this book, I sell an online course called the Publicity Power and Conversion System (super original, right?!).

I teach you all the ins and outs of setting up a webinar. Best of all; I give you a proven and tested PowerPoint template that you literally can just plug in your content and literally produce webinars in a matter of days versus weeks.

I've laid out in the power point template what to talk about at the start, when to start selling, how to start selling and what to include each step of the way so you have a more successful and profitable webinar.

As always; the template is based of real-world webinars that have actually converted and made sales.

I know I can take your planning and design down from 1-2 weeks, to 3-4 days tops to get a webinar up and running.

My goal with the Publicity Power and Conversion System is to radically boost your trajectory to success. Learn from me and my mistakes! Why waste time figuring things out on your own.

I have given you as FastStart pass to learn how to not only get media for your business, how to approach the media to become a writer/ columnist, but also how to set up successful and profitable webinars.

Plus, the program is priced ridiculously cheap! I really should be charging more for it as it's packed with applicable action steps; i.e. no fluff! Plus, it's based off over 14 years in business and has real world, proven action steps that have literally made my multi six figures.

You'll recoup your investment from just one to two media features and webinars.

There's more info about all this at the end of this book. Just letting you if you are keen to get things going and implement and compliment everything you are learning in this book!

Making Sales
Producing Profitable Webinars

Questions to ask yourself to devise a strategy -

1) What am I selling? Which Product / service?

2) Who am I selling to? Ideal audience?

3) How big is my list?

4) How much should I sell my product /service for?

5) What are my financial goals / month?

6) Based on my current list size, will I meet this goal?

Work backwards to work out how many people you need to sell to, ensuring you hit this goal.

7) How can I increase this list?

8) Is there an upsell after this 'webinar sell' to increase my profits?

In addition to these questions, ask;

9) Reiterate - Who is my target audience – a new audience or current one based off my database?

10) Pre and Post Webinar Process – what will you do before and after the webinar to boost sales?

Before we delve deeper into the above questions, keep the following in mind:

Statistics for Potential Sales – these are just conservative averages for examples sake. Actual numbers will vary in your own business.

Based on your list -
20% of people open the email for the webinar.
35% of these will register for your webinar
50% of people will attend your webinar
10% of people could buy from your webinar
Follow up will produce even more sales

For example – say your list has 1000 people on it

1000 people on your database to send info on your webinar to
200 will open our email
70 people will register for your email
35 people will attend the webinar
3-4 people will buy from your webinar
Follow up can produce additional sales.

Webinar Strategy

What am I selling? Which Product / service?

This is your time to get clear on what you intend to sell via your webinar. If like most businesses, you have a range of products and/or services.

I'll use one of my businesses to walk you through the questions.

1) What am I selling? Which Product / service?

I am selling an online course teaching an entrepreneur how to get their own free publicity and media exposure and also how to produce high converting and profitable webinars.

2) Who am I selling to? Ideal audience?

My ideal audience are 24-50-year-old women who are entrepreneurs, running service-based businesses and split between being a total newbie in business, to having run their business for at least 3 years.

3) How big is my list?

My list is approximately 3200 people who have come through as showing specific interest in this topic of conversion and gaining media/publicity exposure.

4) **How much should I sell my product /service for on the webinar?**

On the limited time webinar, I sell this online program for only $997, whereas it retails at $1500 t0 $2000 elsewhere.

5) **What are my financial goals / month?**

For this business, I want to make at least $15,000 per month.

6) **Based on my current list size, will I meet this goal?**

Use the following statistics –

My list size 3200

20% of people open the email for the webinar = 640

35% of this will register for the webinar = 224

50% of people will attend the webinar = 112

10% of people could buy from the webinar = 11 sales

11 sales x $997 = $10,900 approximately (less after expenses, fees, advertising costs etc.)

I won't meet my goal based on the current list size. I need to get more people into the funnel.

How can I increase this list to reach this goal?

Do podcasts, run Facebook Ads, write for magazines, get a media feature for this book etc....

Is there an upsell after this 'webinar sell' to increase my profits?

Currently, no. I can look to add on coaching services to increase profits and sell other resources on specific aspects around conversion.

Hopefully all this gives you an idea of how to plan out your webinar strategy. I could write a whole book on Profitable Webinars alone! It's a meaty and detailed topic, which is the reason why I created an online course around this topic.

The above tips will give you a good head start though.

Remember; the aim of your webinar is to make sales. To do this, you need to convey expertise, you need to then address a problem in their lives and educate them on it AND then you need to show how your product/service is the solution to their problem.

All of the above are the main components to a successful webinar.

Hit on these and you can virtually print money!

Too many webinar hosts miss the mark because they blabble on and on about their business without either defining why they are an expert and/or they forget to educate the viewer and share something of value.

So, follow these 4 steps when designing your webinar:

Define what YOU want from the webinar – to push people down a sales funnel, to bring in new leads, or to make immediate sales.

Define immediately why your potential audience should listen to you. State this clearly at the start of the webinar. You can even say, 'Here's why you should watch this webinar and listen to what I have to say…" Remember to brag about any media features!

Design your webinar content around a problem you know your potential audience currently have. i.e. 'Struggling to lose weight after 35 years old? Learn 3 key lifestyle tips proven to work…"

Be deliberate about the portion of the webinar where you will sell your product / services. You need to plan this out in fine detail. Don't leave anything to chance! Sell your booty off and follow up, follow up, follow up.

We've covered a lot in this book. You have two parts; How to Get Media Coverage and How to Create Profitable Webinars.

I recommend you start with the first part and focus your efforts on getting some media coverage wins under your belt.

If you want to Fast Start your Success and have me walk you through from scratch how to get Media Coverage and Design a Winner Webinar, then I have a great offer for you....

Introducing the
'PublicityPower
and Conversion System'

Online course that literally lays out Step-By-Step how rapidly gain media coverage for your business and also how to create Profitable Webinars from scratch.

Join the online program, then email me the Quote '1MCSBook22'

(E: info@nalishapatel.com) and I will offer you 1 x BONUS 60-minute phone coaching session and 1 x Email Session (total value $1497) with me completely free as part of this special book offer. *

I will even share my contacts and resources with you, helping you get featured, faster!

This is truly invaluable.

I will personally walk you through the techniques and strategies you'll learn on the online program, even giving you a head-start with my best contacts in the media and publishing industry. Value of this; invaluable!

On the Publicity Power and Conversion System;

Learn the Secrets to Ignite your Sales and Get More Clients EASILY and FAST using Webinars that Actually Convert, Free Media and Publicity to Increase Credibility and the Ability to Gain Thousands of Leads per month, for free.

Nothing is B.S. I stand by the fact that everything I teach is real world and proven techniques that actually bring in results and profits.

Media and Publicity Training

- Gain Free Leads through Media Exposure and Publicity! I will show you how, step by step.
- You will learn how to pitch for success.
- How to literally have journalists and writers contacting you
- The #1 way to get your pitch out to the right people
- What to do before, during and after your media blast / feature to maximize profits and radically boost sales.
- My #1 tip for what you need in your media feature to actually ensure you get leads and actually make money.

- Samples of my most successful pitches and templates to formulate your own.

Converting and Profitable Webinars

- Specifically Learn Simple Webinar Creation for Conversion - Full PowerPoint Template Provided So You Produce Webinars Easily and Fast! This alone is worth getting the program.
- What to add and write in your pre and post webinar emails to push sales.
- You'll learn how to sell, what to say and what to do on the webinar to help boost sales
- What to do before, during and after the webinar to radically boost sales
- Sample webinars provided with a complete walk-thru so you can follow the steps for your own webinar
- What platforms to use to create and market your webinars

Nothing is Theory.

All strategies have been PROVEN to actually work in the real world.

GO TO:

http://www.nalishapatel.com/ppsalespage/

to JOIN TODAY FOR THIS SPECIAL OFFER!

BONUS - Join the online program, then email me the Quote 1MCSBook22

(E: info@nalishapatel.com) and I will offer you 1 x BONUS 60-minute phone coaching session and 1 x Email Session (total value $1497) with me completely free as part of this special book offer. *

I will even share my contacts and resources with you, helping you get featured, faster! This is invaluable.

*To be used within 3 months of purchasing the program. 60-minute Phone Coaching Session and 1 x Email session – questions and reply.

Appendix

Appearing on my first magazine cover! This UK based small business magazine brought in a minimal amount of leads and didn't lead to any sales or actual money as far as I could tell, but it lent a lot of credibility and the ability to brag about being on the cover of a magazine.

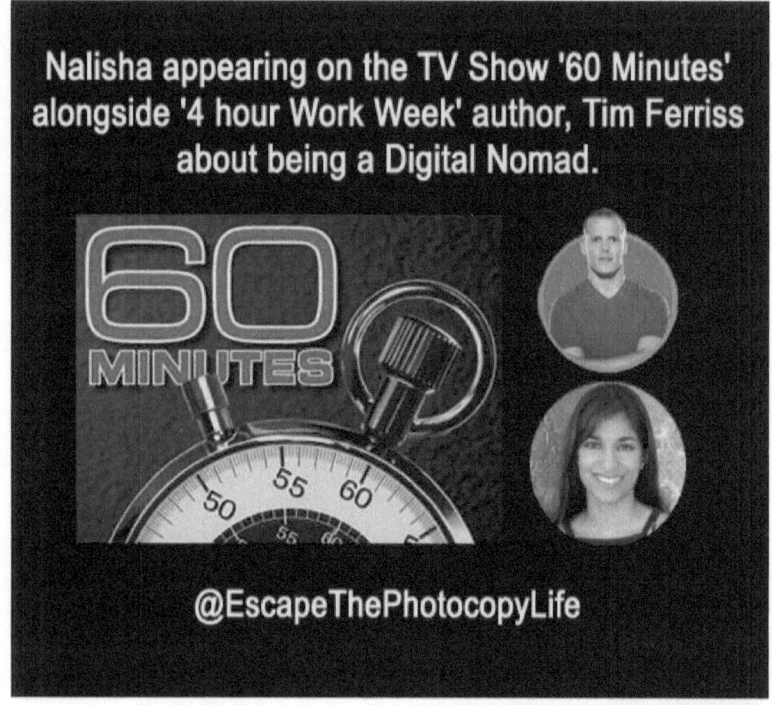

My husband Janak and I were featured on the current affairs TV Show, '60 Minutes', alongside bestselling author and lifehacker, Tim Ferriss, about being Digital Nomads. The TV show was a major credibility booster. Aligning with well-known TV Shows and media outlets radically boost credibility and trust.

THE 1 MINUTE CONVERSION SECRET

Featured on the Entrepreneur.com home page as a featured article was very cool. As mentioned in the book, this article did not bring in leads nor add to my revenue. It was done solely to boost credibility and to have the ability to say, 'As featured on Entrepreneur.com.' Bragging rights have their place!

Featured in Australian Women's Health Magazine (with the gorgeous Jennifer Aniston on the cover). Sharing some of what I eat in a day and cheat meals. Again; done purely for bragging rights in my niche of health and wellness. This particular blast did nothing in terms of leads nor boosting profits. Pick and choose which media features to do. A mix is a good way to rapidly boost credibility.

Featured in the Sunday Star Times in New Zealand about being Digital Nomads – building our online businesses while we travel the world. This feature brought in a lot of emails and enquiries about our online programs. I didn't measure if they led to sales.

The infamous NEXT media feature – 4-page spread that literally changed my business and life. I profited over $88,000 in around 3 months of the feature hitting the newsstands.

Filming for the reality TV Show, 'School of Success'. A fascinating experience! This was a 3-part reality tv / documentary run over 3 weeks about a group of business people (featuring my husband and I and several other business people) who are coached to success. If you squint really hard, you can see my husband and I in the background of the promo shot! This boosted credibility and exposure, and when coupled with other media features out there at the time brought in new business.

2-page spread in Lucky Break magazine. This magazine brought in a few enquiries about our online programs as the article was all about us being Digital Nomads and traveling the world.

6-week feature in Woman's Day Magazine as the Personal Trainer/Fitness Advisor, taking 4 women through 6 weeks of personal training and lifestyle coaching as part of a big Nivea Campaign. This 6-week feature in this nationwide magazine attracted a lot of attention and brought in a flood of new leads and profits.

Interviewed for Yahoo Travel about being a Digital Nomad

Interviewed for a short segment on ONE NEWS TV SHOW (leading NZ TV evening news show) as an expert Personal Trainer about BMI and their validity in health and wellness.

Interviewed by news.com.au about being a Digital Nomad, with the story being picked up by WAKE UP, a leading morning TV Show in Australia. The host recapped our article and shared various travel images. This story and TV segment lead to many inquiries and interest in our business and also requests from other news sites in the UK and NZ to run the story.

NALISHA PATEL

Article in NZ Herald, featured on the main news site, about my weight loss story. This story along with Daily Mail, lead to over $11,000 in sales.

THE 1 MINUTE CONVERSION SECRET

The New Zealand Herald

2nd page of the NZ herald (#1 newspaper in NZ) – story about our life as Digital Nomads. This story was also placed on their website. This story lead to a speaking opportunity, a request to appear on a morning talk show, inquiries for our online business program, and requests to discuss other business opportunities.

NALISHA PATEL

Use Your Bucket List to Design Your Life – feature article on how we became Digital Nomads. Also featured a video interview.

Quoted in Nature and Health Magazine

THE 1 MINUTE CONVERSION SECRET

Nalisha Patel—Weight-loss Transformation Story

The big Daily Mail feature that brought in over 440 free leads and lead to over $11,000 in sales (along with NZ Herald)

Some of magazines I've written / columnist for

Writing multiple times for various magazines in different niches to gain credibility and exposure.

About the Author

Nalisha Patel is a Media/Marketing Coach, Online Health and Wellness Trainer, and also a Digital Nomad.

After appearing in over 60+ different media outlets, including: Entrepreneur.com, Women's Health Magazine, Sydney Morning Herald, The Huffington Post, Yahoo Travel, DailyMail UK, and the TV Show, '60 Minutes', alongside life hacker and bestselling author, Tim Ferriss, Nalisha can help teach you about the power of utilizing free media and publicity to gain leads and increased profits.

Traveling the world with her husband since 2011 as a Digital Nomad, while building online businesses, Nalisha wants to help you build up a profitable business, using smart and little-used strategies that have been proven to work in the real world.

She built up one of Australasia's' Largest 'In-home' mobile fitness company, with Licensed Personal Trainers throughout Australia and New Zealand. She's since turned that business into a 100% online one, now operating in over 13 countries worldwide.

After operating her unique online health & fitness programs for over 8 years, she now helps other Entrepreneurs Digitize their knowledge into Digital Products, so they too can travel the world.

She is the author of, 'How to Escape the Photocopy Life', is the #1 Digital Nomad Personal Trainer in the world and is an award-winning Young Entrepreneur.

Nalisha's straight-shooting viewpoints on wealth, wellness, mindset, marketing and business have made her a valuable resource for various media seeking insights into these topics.

She regularly appears in the media and urges other small business owners and entrepreneurs to utilize the power of free ways to generate leads, build trust and strive for increased profits.

She now focuses primarily on running her PublicityPower and Conversion Marketing Program, helping entrepreneurs gain free publicity and media to radically boost their businesses.